Cost Reduction Strategies
and Lean Thinking Techniques
for all Companies

By

Ammar D. Halloum

Cost Reduction Strategies, And Lean Thinking Techniques For All Companies

© 2008 Ammar D. Halloum. All Rights Reserved

No part of this book may be reproduced or transmitted in any form or by any means, graphic, electronic or mechanical, including photocopying, recording, typing, or by any information storage retrieval system, without the written permission of the publisher.

Publisher's Cataloging-In-Publication Data
(Prepared by The Donohue Group, Inc.)

Halloum, Ammar D.
  Cost reduction strategies and lean thinking techniques for all companies / by Ammar D. Halloum.
    p. ; cm.
  Includes bibliographical references.
  ISBN-13: 978-0-9801197-1-8

1. Cost control. 2. Production management. 3. Manufacturing processes. 4. Labor productivity. 5. Organizational effectiveness. I. Title.

HD47.3 .H35 2008
658.15/52

Published by A to Z Publishing

P. O. Box 26662

Tempe, Arizona 85285

USA

Publisher@atozpublisher.com

www.atozpublisher.com

ISBN: 978-0-9801197-1-8

Book cover design by Thunderbird Graphics
Book layout design by A to Z Publishing
Editing by A to Z Publishing

Printed in the United States of America

ACKNOWLEDGEMENTS

I am extremely grateful to my father who gave me the encouragement, and inspiration to continue my higher education in order to contribute to humanity by becoming an educator like him. I am indebted to my mother who taught me patience and persistence, which was needed to do in depth research and to document all the techniques that have been applied through out my career. Finally my friends played a great role in providing me the support needed to meeting the challenges of producing this book while going through many difficulties of life.

DEDICATION

I dedicate this book with gratitude and love to my parents who encouraged me throughout this endeavor. I also dedicate this book to my four wonderful children, who have been away from me physically, but present in my heart while doing the research and writing of this book.

CONTENT

	PAGE
Introduction	1
CHAPTER I OVERVIEW of COST REDUCTION,	3
AND LEAN THINKING TECHNIQUES	

1.1   Overview

1.1.2 Definition of lean manufacturing
1.1.3 Approach to Lean Manufacturing
1.1.4 Training
1.2   Statement of the Problem
1.3   Potential Benefits and Contributions
1.3.1 Benefits
1.3.2 Contributions
1.4   Research Outcome
1.5   Organization of the Book

CHAPTER II   IDENTIFYING THE ISSUES   15
   2.1   Introduction
2.2.1 Organization Issues
2.2.2 The Steps of Leading Organization Change
2.2.3 Modifying the business design
2.2.4 Competition Choices for a Lean Enterprise
2.3   Stopping Bad Things from Happening to Good Companies
2.3.1 Selecting the right mix of work force
2.3.2 Getting the organization to face the external environment
2.3.3 Insisting on "out of the box" market research or exploration
2.4   Concentrating on improvement.

2.4.1 Maintaining Productivity involves balancing many factors
2.4.2 Mobilizing Leadership

2.5   Value chain shortcuts
2.6   The Art and Practice of Japanese Management
2.6.1   Mass Production Factors
2.6.2   Costs Associated with Mass Production
2.7   Re-engineering for Growth
2.7.1 Need for Leadership and empowerment
2.7.2 Building Individual and Team Pride
2.7.3 Strategy 1: Getting strategic choices made
2.7.4 Strategy 2: How to keep the implementation process from spinning out of control -
2.7.5 Involvement of the chief executive or the division manager
2.7.6 A Modest Formula for Reengineering
2.7.7 Identifying Cost Areas
2.7.8 Cost Benefit Analysis
2.7.9 Steps of Cost-benefit analysis
2.7.10 An Action Plan/ Getting Started
2.7.11 Area Managers Action Plan
2.7.12 Evaluating Progress
2.7.13 Reasons for becoming lean
2.7.14 Next Steps for lean thinking
2.7.15 Cost Reduction in Progress
2.7.16 CEO and Top Management Level
2.7.17 Managers Level

CHAPTER III   AN OVERVIEW OF THE TECHNIQUE   47
3.1   Introduction
3.2   Structure of the Technique
3.3   Procedure of the Technique
3.4   Dividing the Target

CHAPTER IV   DETERMINATION AND FORMULATION   55
                OF THE COST REDUCTION PLAN
4.1   Introduction
4.2   Determination of Cost Reduction Target
4.3   Formulation of the Cost Reduction Plan
4.4   Formulation of the implementation methodology
4.5   Implementation Diagram
4.5   Monitoring the Cost Reduction Progress

4.6   Cost Reduction Road Map

CHAPTER V   CONCLUSIONS AND FURTHER RESEARCH 67
5.1 Summary
5.2 Conclusions
5.3 Contributions
5.3 Further Research

REFERENCES   71

APPENDICIES

APPENDIX A   75

Sample of Cost Reduction Projects
Progress Report on Engineering Projects

APPENDIX B   79

Cost Reduction Progress Report

Cost Reduction Strategies *Ammar Halloum*

Introduction

To overcome the existing overspending and lack of quality process management in manufacturing and production companies, there is a need to identify a cost reduction model and to provide techniques that helps the identification, and implementation of cost reduction projects. In this book, cost reduction projects are identified and implementation techniques are developed.

The objective of the presented approach is to help the transition from traditional spending approach in any company to a dynamic lean production environment utilizing lean thinking, and quality process management. Several fundamental requirements for the objectives are discussed. The major features of the approach are establishing cost reduction goals, identifying projects and opportunities in a fast cycle time utilizing quality process management.

An application of the techniques was tested on a high tech, semiconductor manufacturing company. The cost reduction opportunities were identified and cost reduction projects were applied. A quality process management was established to guide the identification, and implementation of these projects. In addition, a state of the art model was devised to track and measure the implementation of all cost reduction projects. The author of this book helped a company save $185 Million Dollars in one year utilizing the techniques and disciplines found in this book. Also, the author of this book has done his PhD dissertation in the same subject, which took years of research, analysis, and application.

The presented techniques have been proven to be valid for the mentioned purposes and applicable in principal to any sizable company. This research will contribute to future lean thinking and quality process management.

CHAPTER 1

An Overview Of Cost Reduction, And Lean Thinking

Rapid growth and high profit in manufacturing have drifted companies from watching their spending. Engaging in competition, product improvement, and building wealth, companies tend to disregard its spending strategies. Companies operations tend to be less efficient, and care less about negotiating prices with suppliers.

There is a great recognition that products costs, waste of resources, and production lead-time have to be reduced in order to survive in the world marketplace. As competition increases in the 21st century, the enterprises that will flourish will be those that can produce, improve and distribute products the most timely and at the least cost. This puts corporate of the world on notice: *Think lean or perish*. Running your company as efficiently as possible has become critical in recent years and even more urgent during the struggles of today's economy. Some alternative approaches are beginning to help companies implement Lean Manufacturing improvements quickly, inexpensively, and without overburdening staff resources.

In today's rapidly changing world the principles of Strategic Planning and Strategic Thinking have changed. The traditional "once a year" management planning session to review plans is no longer acceptable. Long-range visioning exercises that are rarely translated into everyday activities are of little value in today's business world.

Strategic planning and thinking must be agile, lean, aggressive and responsive. Strategic plans that resemble a marketing advertisement are of little value. Business plans beyond three years are too much guesswork and detract from what everyone should be thinking. If an organization does not have clearly defined, assigned, focused and accountable goals and responsibilities, the achievement of objectives is nearly impossible. In order to succeed, everyone must be on the same page. A company must have a plan and it must be followed throughout the organization. Progress must be constantly measured. The plan must be continuously evaluated and updated. The teams must be skilled and trained in utilizing companies' resources efficiently and effectively. The process must be in place to support and facilitate lean manufacturing. It is essential to integrate these into a framework that focuses on appropriate use of tools and resources to drive breakthrough business results.

1.1.2 Definition of Lean Manufacturing

Lean manufacturing is a proven approach to reduce waste and streamline operations. Lean manufacturing embraces a philosophy of continually increasing the proportion of value added activity of their business through ongoing waste elimination. the guidelines incorporate manufacturing related concepts that have been evolving over the past ten years and are becoming standard business practices in the areas of Total Quality Management, Enterprise Resource Planning, Activity Based Costing and Lean Manufacturing. A lean thinking approach provides companies with tools to survive in a global market that demands higher quality, faster delivery and lower prices. Specifically,

- Lean manufacturing dramatically reduces the waste chain.
- Lean manufacturing reduces inventory and floor space requirements.
- Lean manufacturing creates more robust production systems.
- Lean manufacturing develops appropriate material delivery systems.
- Lean manufacturing improves layouts for increased flexibility.

In short, lean thinking is lean because it provides a way to do more and more with less and less—less human effort, less equipment, less time, and less space—while coming closer and closer to providing customers with exactly what they want.

The Lean Manufacturing System requires the design and continuous improvement of the manufacturing process including production, materials management, design engineering, marketing, customer service, all employees and the supply chain. Lean organizations are capable of producing high quality products economically in lower volumes and bringing them to market faster than mass producers. A lean organization can make twice the product with twice the quality in half the time and space, at half the cost. Lean Manufacturing is about operating the most efficient and effective organization possible with the least cost and zero waste. Today, "lean" manufacturing concepts are widely accepted as the most effective way to manage manufacturing processes and attain a high degree of worker competency and dedication.

1.1.3 Approach to Lean Manufacturing

Lean production is aimed at the elimination of waste in every area of production including customer relations, product design, supplier networks and factory management. Its goal is to incorporate less human effort, less inventory, less time to develop products, and less space to become highly responsive to customer demand while producing top quality products in the most efficient and economical manner possible. "Lean production systems require a major change in how companies operate their businesses. Lean production systems not only require changes in technical systems, but also necessitate changes in the organizational infrastructure and corporate culture as well."

This book pursues the development of a comprehensive approach for the design of lean production systems. Attempts in the past on improving production have focused on specific areas of manufacturing. This book is taking a holistic approach at designing manufacturing systems according to the principles of Lean Production, which include:

- Establishing a vision
- Thinking about the future
- Assessing core capabilities
- Developing a strategy
- Competition analysis
- Strategic improvement cycle
- Standardization
- Organizing cost reduction teams
- Assessing financial impacts
- Cost reduction Team activities
- Team implementation activities
- Plan adherence
- Measurement techniques
- Reevaluation of the plan

1.1.4 Training:

For industrial companies, trained employees are the key to success. Their level of knowledge has a direct impact on continuous improvement, customer satisfaction, and increased profitability. Training strategies in an industrial environment are difficult to develop, costly to deliver and often impossible to execute because of resource constraints. Companies webs enable customized training, focused content to focus specifically on turning training strategy into deliverable knowledge.

Emphasis need to be on a wide range of capabilities, efficiency and productivity improvement, employee development, management empowerment, quality improvement and web technology solutions that touch the right part of the business at the right time.

1.2 Statement of the Problem:

In a rapidly growing demand for technology, Semiconductor manufacturing companies might grow fat where spending is not watched carefully. The absence of lean manufacturing and appropriate process management causes companies to decline. When the economy slows down, only companies with lean manufacturing can resist the impact and continue operation under harsh economic conditions.

Companies struggle for many reasons, including the following: Inventory build, slow reaction to the market, under or over production, low yield, over spending, obscure supply chain, excessive waste, dissatisfied customers, employees inadequate training, poor process management, and absence of a robust management information system. There is a need to maximize design flexibility, process capabilities, and waste elimination, while always meeting customer needs and expectations. Building leaner business system will safeguard the company through harsh economic conditions. As a company grows, more work is needed to keep the company lean.

The need for transitioning from the traditional manufacturing process to lean manufacturing has been discussed. However, there has not been a definite listing of cost reduction projects and identification of the quality process management to support lean thinking. There are many obstacles in the way of transitioning to a lean manufacturing environment. Changing the culture to implement cost reduction in every facet of the business is one of the major difficulties. Transitioning from the traditional process management to an agile process management is another difficulty. In addition, excluding the hierarchical organizational structure, and assigning tasks to resources in a cross-functional team structure is a major problem to be solved. After teams are formed, the task management through team interaction is also one of the problems, which should be solved.

Problems in the application of cost reduction are mostly involved with managers, engineers, suppliers, tasks, time and their interaction. Transforming a traditional organization into a fast cycle time competitor requires a systematic organizational change strategy combined with cycle time reduction methods and tools. The strategy has to define what the organization has to let go of as well as what it must simultaneously add to reduce cycle time. Under the desired circumstances, the constitution of quality process management may help reduces the time in implementing cost reduction projects.

The results of the cost reduction projects will be measured against the initial target and benchmarked against the performance of other factories, and other competitor companies. To come up with an accurate benchmarking, the cost reduction target will be set in both total amounts of cost reduction and cost per produced unit. Since companies may have different production volume or loading, the cost per unit is calculated to be the total spending of the factory divided by the loading (the number of units produced by the factory).

1.3 Potential Benefits and Contributions

1.3.1 Benefits

Several benefits are expected to be learned:

1. A lean environment and culture can be created for the improvement of effectiveness and efficiency of the operation.
2. The production cost, and the product lead-time will be reduced.
3. Profit is increased, and the vulnerability to drastic losses is decreased.
4. Employees feel more secure, and their jobs are saved in an economy slow down.

5. An environment of discipline and self-watching toward spending will be promoted.

6. Individuals within their teams collaborate to achieve cost reduction goals.

7. Teams will compete to achieve favorable results.

1.3.2 Contributions

This study develops and tests a rigorous methodology that compares cost reduction approaches and achievements to solve manufacturing problems. It provides the possibility of the practical identification and implementation of lean manufacturing projects. These projects save manufacturing companies a lot of money and therefore balance companies' growth and downsizing. The balance in spending will have a positive impact on employees' job stability.

1.4 Research Outcome

This book attempts to identify and implement cost reduction projects to solve manufacturing problems, especially in a slow economy. The quality process management needed to identify and implement these projects will help the organization apply lean thinking in all areas of operation. Therefore, the study in this book will present a state of the art cost reduction model, and an implementation technique to help manufacturing companies reduce their cost. None manufacturing companies may benefit from this research by using a significant portion of the cost reduction projects, the lean thinking approach, and the implementation technique.

1.5 Organization of the Book

This book is structured as follows. Chapter II presents a survey of the current techniques related to lean manufacturing, cost reduction, and quality process management in manufacturing. The manufacturing issues include:

1. The organization,
2. People,
3. Cost reduction projects,
4. Cross-functional teams,
5. Information technology, and
6. Interaction and integration issues.

The cost reduction projects will be identified, and a roadmap will be created to identify the implementation process.
Chapter III introduces the necessary reasons for designing a cost reduction model. The detailed articulations of the technique are presented in Chapter IV, which contains the structure of the proposed process management technique, the construction of the cost reduction model, the roadmap specifications, the information technology tools

needed to support the model, and strategies to monitor and control the implementation of the model.

Finally, Chapter V presents the summary of the strategies and the implementation of lean thinking, and other future study and research issues.

CHAPTER 2

IDENTIFYING THE ISSUES

2.2 Introduction

This chapter covers several issues associated with lean manufacturing. These issues include manufacturing spending, cost reduction projects, and quality process management needed to support the identification and implementation of these projects. The literature contains ample research on various single aspects of lean manufacturing, however few studies attempt to link these aspects together to provide a bigger picture about how or whether lean manufacturing works. There is a dearth of information on a holistic, and comprehensive cost reduction planning, and implementation approach.

In the section of manufacturing issues, the organization, people and integration problems are tackled. The existing problems in organizations, the change of the organizational structures and people in manufacturing environment are all discussed.

In the section on Stopping Bad Things from Happening to Good Companies, several ideas are introduced. These ideas consist of having the company select the right mix of work force, face the external environment, and insist on pursuing out of the box research.

In the section on Concentrating on Improvement, the manufacturing trend that demands the transition to lean thinking from traditional manufacturing is explained. The lean manufacturing concept and definition, cases of implementation, and benefits and guidelines are explored. Several factors that affect lean manufacturing are discussed in the later part of this section. In addition, an overview of the style of Japanese management in manufacturing is introduced.

In the section of Reengineering Growth, the research areas associated with selecting strategic choices, putting the C.E.O. or the top manager in charge, a modest formula to cost reduction, forming teams and mapping the process. The last section presents techniques that include identifying cost areas, stages cost benefit analysis, an action plan to get started, evaluating progress, next steps for lean thinking and reasons for becoming lean.

2.2 Organization Issues

Over the last twenty years, the western market has changed from primarily domestic competition to global competition. Business strategies, which were once effective, no longer apply to this highly competitive and volatile market. The changing in global market requires organizations to have scope and vision beyond the single business unit. An organization's success will be formulated by their ability to develop core competencies that generate new products. A company's core competencies consist of an amalgamation of skills, technologies, and knowledge, which can provide a company with a unique advantage in the market place. One of these core competencies can be lean organization.

Major, painful cost reductions are inevitable when business designs become rigid and lose their economic relevance. The best defense is to evaluate and update the strategy and the design of the product frequently. Crafting the right design for the next phase of value migration must rise to the top of management's agenda.

2.2.1 Leading Organization Change

Without an appropriate vision, a transformation effort can easily dissolve into a list of confusing, incompatible, and time-consuming projects that go in the wrong direction or nowhere at all. To be effective, a method designed to alter strategies, reengineer processes, or improve quality must address these barriers and address them well. The process has eight stages, each of which is associated with one of the eight fundamental errors that undermine transformation efforts.

The steps of Leading Organization Change:

1. Establishing a sense of urgency,

2. Creating the guiding coalition,
3. Developing a vision and strategy,
4. Communicating the change vision,
5. Empowering a broad base of people to take action,
6. Generating short-term wins,
7. Consolidating gains and producing even more change, and
8. Institutionalizing new approaches in the culture.

2.2.2 Modifying the business design before the company is forced to do so

The business redesign process is best started early, before companies' freedom becomes dangerously constrained. It is vital that producers accept the challenge of redefinition, because this is often the key to finding more customers, and the ability to find more customers and sales very quickly is critical to the success of lean thinking.

The most important task in specifying value, once the product is defined, is to determine a target cost based on the amount of resources and effort required to make a product of given specification and capabilities if all the currently visible "muda" were removed from the process. Doing this is the key to squeezing out the waste. *Muda* is a Japanese word, which means waste, specifically any human activity, which uses resources but creates no value.

Because the target is certain to be far below the costs borne by competitors, the lean enterprise has choices to gain completive edge in competitive markets:

Competition Choices for a Lean Enterprise:

1. **Reduce prices** (another way to increase sales volume and utilize freed-up resources); Add features or capabilities to the product (which should also increase sales);

2. **Add services** to the physical product to create additional value (and jobs);

3. **Expand the distribution** and service network (again increasing sales, although with a time lag); or

4. **Take projects to underwrite new products**, which will increase sales in the longer term.

2.3 Stopping Bad Things from Happening to Good Companies

2.3.1 Selecting the right mix of work force

The number and quality of employees are important, but more must be considered. The relationship of employees to their employer and the trend of the employees must also be managed. Every organization needs some staff to support the lines people, those, who actually sell, service and produce, but having too many definitely contributes to calcification.

Staff growth should be below the lesser of profit, sales or line employment growth. Like total employment, it should be benchmarked against the leanest similar company. Requests for additional staff hiring should be subject to more stringent controls and treated more cautiously than requests for line hires. Hiring at all levels should include managers from other industries to encourage open-thinking systems. Pruning and the right kind of hiring at all levels insure a more balanced, flexible, change-responsive work force.

Finally, *a company must hire "outside the box" thinkers as well as those who can do the present work better.* The goal, again, is a dynamic balance. But some companies attract more than their share of out of the box thinkers, and others hire only those who think as their managers do. Competent interviewers apparently distinguish between those who advocate the company way and those who might constructively challenge it. The out-of-the-box thinkers are valuable players on your team; their creativity is contagious.

As value migrates, energizing the organization requires reallocating human resources from traditionally powerful functions to those that will be critical to future success. Relative importance will shift to discovery, development and account management for key customers.

The value migration process determines not only which functions will rise in importance, but also which new skills and technologies are necessary to meet future customer needs. Professionals with future-relevant skills must become a part of the organizational fabric. Without integrating new skills into the company's business design, that design will become increasingly irrelevant to customers.

The above actions help create a work force, including a management team, capable of dealing with the discontinuous change that value migration implies. The team must identify the drivers of value migration as it approaches, and must understand the mechanisms by which the drivers interact with one another. The team must also form the company's response early. Leaders can help in many ways to ensure timely implementation.

2.3.2 Getting the organization to face the external environment

Here are considerations in facing the external environment:

1. **Hiring Outside the Box:** It is vitally important to hire people with different experience and the capability to think outside conventional confines.

2. **Raising the Market Share**: External goals related to the marketplace such as share of market, quality of market share, customer satisfaction and customer retention provide the right type of scope setting.

3. **Raising the Bar:** Constant scrutiny of performance against such goals is an important factor in achieving good results.

4. **Using and Advance Manufacturing Systems:** The agile environment demands the use of advanced manufacturing information management technology such as Manufacturing Resources Planning (MRP II) and Manufacturing Execution Systems (MES).

2.3.3 Insisting on "out of the box" market research or exploration

Exploring the truth includes asking tough questions directly to toughest customers. It is necessary to hear the real criticism that people don't like to hear. These negative remarks, or strange demands, are very important to changing companies' approaches and strategies. When it comes to customer's satisfaction, Companies' main goal must not only be meeting the customer's expectations, but to make the customer successful and appreciative of the products' value.

2.4 Concentrating on improvement.

The quality movement in its many forms has been, and is, fundamental. But too often it focuses on doing the old things (in a strategic sense) better. Value migration puts a premium on doing new things. A major tension in the organization is between doing new things and doing the old things better. Both are important. A strategy focusing only on continuous improvement is dangerously incomplete. Once the improvement occurred leading to productivity and efficiency, maintaining the improvement is as important as the improvement itself.

2.4.1 Maintaining productivity involves balancing many factors:

1. Operator training,
2. Equipment maintenance,
3. Ensuring quality control, and
4. Accurate production scheduling.

Cross-training of operators helps maintain productivity even when a key operator is missing.

2.4.2 Mobilizing Leadership

Implicit in the recommended actions for responding to the need and ability to move is the crucial importance of asserting leadership. Effective leaders look beyond their organizations toward their customers and competitors. Key groups along with distribution channels and business partners determine the destiny of the company. These leaders, and their top managers, will also look deeply into their organizations, listening to and talking with production workers and field sales representatives. Those production workers and sales representatives may understand quality problems and customers' needs better than the manufacturing managers and marketing managers. Effective leaders and their top managers will listen to those who actually use their company's offerings, and they will ask the hard questions. Overall, effective leaders and their organizations are poised for the future.

Maintaining external responsiveness and internal suppleness to enable a company to serve and shape markets demands a remarkable constellation of talents. And a little luck along the way is always welcome. Because these tasks are difficult, most businesses fail. They don't all necessarily go bankrupts; rather, they fail to reach their full potential. History shows, however, that the job can be done right. Success can be sustained over long periods, and leaders can lead. Companies can move before they must. Leaders who assert themselves and face the truth are found to be successful.

2.5 Value Chain Shortcuts

The key business strategy on the new continent is to bypass the value chain and shorten the links between the company and the customer. Since the interface between the company and the customer is crucial, the customer should be able to order directly from the provider without having to go through an intermediary. It is also essential to have a lean supply chain system to cut the middleman, and to expedite the delivery of parts, and raw material. Companies are investing in software, hiring consultants, and reconfiguring their physical supply chains in order to capture the promised returns from lean supply chain management. Yet the returns from these investments can be elusive. What these companies may not realize is that it's not about expense reduction or profit enhancement—it's about creating capacity for growth.

Creating electronic links to customers and suppliers saves companies a lot of money and makes it easier and more convenience to process. Peter Solvik, chief information officer at network products-maker Cisco Systems, reports that Cisco saves $200 each time a customer doesn't call its support center. Where do customers with problems get solutions? Companies' websites conveniently provide solutions. Each month, tens of thousand of customers log on to get answers to questions. Solvik expects savings of over $100 million over a year.

Cisco Systems' automated purchase process was used by 70 percent of its customers to place orders via the Web. As a result, there is no need for a traditional sales force. Cisco has more than 120 partners in its Internet router production process who act together - procuring, producing, shipping, and repairing as a single, virtual company. Customers place orders directly into an "Electronic Retrieval Process" system that selects suppliers and assemblers. Even the engineering function is integrated into the system; when a customer designs a router, the product is fitted to his or her needs by Cisco's design department using its database of customer-developed specifications.

The companies that use this platform join Cisco's partnership and become, in effect, part of the corporate nervous system. From the customers' perspective, the platform is seamless; whether a router is made at a Cisco plant or by a partner company makes no difference to them. Cisco's computers test all finished products in order to protect its brand name. The system saves Cisco $450 million per year. Replacing the workforce with technology is a big step toward a lean company.

The inventory turnover is an important factor in cost reduction. Institute some kind of just-in-time inventory system (both coming and going) so you don't sit on component or-heaven forbid-finished goods any longer than you must. In a competitive market, the prices of finished goods depreciate rapidly, and lose most of their values as products with new capabilities are introduced.

2.6 The Art and Practice of Japanese Management

Despite all the noise in recent years over the concept of "lean" manufacturing, most U.S. companies have not fully incorporated lean techniques into their manufacturing plants, observes Thomas Jackson (2000), a vice president with Productivity Inc., a Portland-based training and publishing firm. Among the reasons why lean concepts haven't been more fully exploited, he says, are a lack of leadership and failure to appreciate the time and resources required for successful implementations. He added most business executives are in an abject state of denial about how long it will take their companies to become lean.

Lean production, consensus and continuous improvement defined Japan's extraordinary postwar industrial success. But lately it has been the countries perceived weak points, such as lifetime employment and over-regulation that have come to the forefront of the debate on Japanese management. But new ideas are emerging with the younger, more flexible generation of Japanese managers, which means there will still be plenty for the outside world to learn from Japan.

Lean production was the offspring of a set of ideas about quality that Japanese businesses first encountered. This procedure challenges the entire basis of mass production, which was (and in many parts of the world still is) the dominant manufacturing philosophy.

2.6.1 Mass Production Depends on Two Factors:

1. Economies of Scale: Factories need to get bigger and bigger to achieve economies of scale.
2. Specialization: Workers, supposedly, need to get more and more specialized in order to do their jobs more efficiently.

2.6.2 Costs Associated with Mass Production:

However, as the Japanese realized, this system also entails two costs. The first is the inability of a classic mass-production system to respond to rapid changes in demand. Mass producers tend to be much keener on keeping standardized designs in production than in experimenting with new products, partly because of the heavy costs of changing the production line and partly because their specialized workers are happiest with what they know. A change in fashion may mean that the factory has to close down for months as machines are re-calibrated and workers retrained. It may also force producers to throw away huge quantities of expensively stored but now obsolete inventory. By the time it is capable of mass-producing the new product, the demand may have changed once again.

The second cost is an unacceptably high rate of faulty products. Large batches make it difficult to detect defects. This means that a defective part may not reveal itself until the finished car finally breaks down. It is easier for the next person on the assembly line to check a small batch. And a worker making only a small batch is likely to feel more like a craftsman and less like a cog in a huge machine.

In fact, the trouble with mass production is that it usually produces its economies of scale by reducing jobs to labor. By contrast, lean production continues to engage at least some of the intellectual gifts of the workers. The employee can see the impact of his workmanship, good or bad, on the company's manufacturing process. Pats on the back from his colleagues result from a job well done.

Lean production also involved rethinking the boundaries of the firm -- in particular its relationship with its suppliers. In the West, automakers have been through two stages. First, they tried to make virtually the entire car themselves, setting up their own parts-making divisions. When the fashion turned against such "vertical integration," Western companies then opted for a second system based on competing suppliers. They provided a large number of suppliers with a detailed drawing of what they wanted and then offered a one-year contract to the supplier who could come up with the best price.

The classic form of Japanese supply-chain management, again pioneered by Toyota, works in a different way. The suppliers can be formally separate companies, or they can be members of the same *keiretsu* (linked by cross-shareholdings). Either way, the parent company treats them as partners, rather than playing them off against one another. The suppliers provide the goods "just in time," in return for long-term relationships with the main manufacturers. Implementing lean thinking, the findings indicate that internal lean manufacturing practices can facilitate Just-in-Time logistics.

Companies cement these relationships by sending mid-career managers to high-level positions in supplier companies or other members of a *keiretsu*. This means all parts of the supply chain can pool resources and also share information -- thus once again cutting-down on time wasting. Even today, Toyota can design and build a car twice as fast as Detroit can.

The emphasis on communal decision-making is evidence that the Japanese have an idiosyncratic approach to leadership. Where American bosses are brash and bullying, their Japanese counterparts are modest and retiring; and where Americans live to make decisions, the Japanese prefer to let decisions make themselves. They like to compare leadership to air necessary for life but invisible and insubstantial. They rise up the corporate ranks by out-conforming their colleagues, religiously putting the group before the individual, and, having reached the top job, lead by consensus rather than command. It is not unusual for leaders to sit in silence throughout much of a meeting, while their underlings debate the pros and cons of policy. The art of leadership is to divine the will of the group, not to electrify the organization with charisma.

It also means that the Japanese have an idiosyncratic approach to forming long-term strategy. In the West, strategy has traditionally been clear and definite, drawn up by professional strategists and written down in formal plans. In Japan, it is a much looser affair, generated by the whole organization and expressed in terms of visions and missions rather than precise plans.

To the Western mind, producing plans like this is a recipe for disaster. But, the Japanese can do it because it fits in with their general approach to employment. The system of lifetime employment means that core workers identify with the long-term future of the company. The habit of rotating people among different departments means that they soon come to think like strategists. And the convention that everybody must start on the shop floor means that senior managers know what is going on in the guts of their organizations.

This skill allows companies to tap into the insights of the bulk of their employees, and insures that one man's hunch can become an entire firm's competitive advantage. The most important trick is to encourage workers to spend as much time as possible together, informally as well as formally. Companies routinely divide workers into teams, often expecting them to stick with the same colleagues for years on end. New recruits work closely with "mentors" or "team leaders," learning far more from them than they do from formal training courses. The point about tacit knowledge is that it is always there; a company does not have to create it, but rather remove the barriers that surround it.

One problem with implicit knowledge is that it is difficult to push across borders, even when people share the same language. Yet while Japanese companies have a fairly bad record at extracting ideas from their foreign subsidiaries, they have also been fairly capable teachers -- particularly when it comes to teaching tacit knowledge about manufacturing.

2.7 Re-engineering for Growth

The next wave is utilizing the tools used in re-engineering for growth must modify and add to the existing tool kit. Classic manufacturing tools have included elimination of duplicated work, de-layering organizations, cutting redundant quality checks, centralizing functions to achieve economies of scale, automation, outsourcing, etc. There is great cost reduction value in the existing tool kit and low cost is still an important component in the value for cost equation.

However, the classic tools will require a different calibration with a focus on growth. For example, a lean, flat organization that is optimized for low cost will be stretched too thin in a renewed growth environment, as new functions, facilities and employees are added. A company optimized for a narrow manufacturing and marketing footprint will fail in a growth mode incorporating global expansion. A decision-making structure that empowers low-level teams could create great risk as new products and services are rolled out. Developing and freeing up the capabilities for growth will require taking some of the stars out of the processes, instead of the deadwood.

The classic tools, applied with a different future perspective, should improve some of these conditions. But simply re-calibrating the old tools will not be enough. New re-engineering tools are required to analyze and realign processes and business systems for growth. It is likely that a number of different processes will find their way onto the priority list, requiring changes far outside the classic re-engineering experience. Growth, especially with a global flavor, will demand new planning and risk assessment capabilities, new information technology systems, new human resource management processes and new product and service development approaches. In some cases, this will require tools and skills in building rather than rebuilding processes. It will also require leveraging lessons learned from other companies that have already been through successful global expansion programs. Companies need to learn about cost reduction's norm in term of amount and time. When reengineering effort promises that the first cost reductions will come in twelve months and they occur as predicted, that's a win.

Developing and delivering capabilities for growth in the new environment will require moving beyond the masters of cost reduction for both internal leadership and external support. In a way, this is "back to the future," as some of the required skills and tools were developed and used in the expansionary 70's and 80's. Nonetheless, the global dynamics of the 90's and the increased pace of change will make it necessary to restore and redevelop those tools in a significant way.

2.7.1 Need for Leadership and Empowerment

Experience has shown that employees have greater respect for those mangers, who share the decision making. Mangers demonstrate their self-confidence in their own position and their confidence in their employees when they empower their staff members. Loyalty grows as employees see their manager on their side. Before you make this significant change in management style, though, you need to prepare your employees.

2.7.2 Building Individual and Team Pride

Staff members develop pride in their work and continue to improve its quality when they see their manager recognizing high-quality performance. High-Value managers are always on the lookout for quality work by their staff members and praise them generously. But high-value managers make it a point to praise not only individual workers, but the department as a whole whenever they can.

Perhaps one of the most innovative approaches to implementing Lean quickly and with minimal downtime, Lean on the Run uses the experience and talents of a Lean Consultant/Facilitator, an assistant, and occasional help from the "team" or staff assigned to the area being improved.

Implementing Lean Manufacturing techniques throughout the company while transferring "Lean Expertise" to the in-house "Improvement Manager" trainee(s) is the goal of this program. Hours of instruction are conducted in a primarily hands-on fashion as the Lean expert teaches, coaches, and collaboratively implements various aspects of Lean Manufacturing throughout the company.

During the repair period, all workers receive in-depth knowledge of the equipment. During the production stage, they are frequently involved in checking the same machinery. This makes them feel like the owners of the equipment, and they often propose and effect improvements in their areas.

2.7.3 Strategy 1: Getting strategic choices made

The legacy processes that are being replaced, by necessity, embedded much of the communication and control in the business processes, and years of learning made this set of business processes very efficient and effective. Most implementations do not recognize and therefore do not capture this organizational efficiency.

Lean production systems deliver low cost, low overhead, highly effective communication and control. For example, when a production process using Japanese visual signals needs more raw materials from a supplier, production workers pull a card and send it to the supplier. The communication and control are built into the process design. Yet United States companies that are implementing lean production techniques often put a firewall between the two, not recognizing that this undermines both. The right answer is to recognize the decision the company is facing and make the decision explicit for all the company's efforts.

2.7.4 Strategy 2: How to keep the implementation process from spinning out of control - put the C.E.O. or the top manager in charge

The new commandment for senior management is "Put the chief executive officer in charge." We hasten to add that we are not referring to the usual "first commandment" of getting support from the top. Putting the chief executive officer in charge defines a different level of involvement in the implementation process.

The business case for implementing a lean system is invariably built around significant cost reductions and improved capabilities. The cost savings are based on reduced legacy information technology costs as well as decreased indirect labor, direct labor and inventory costs. Improved capabilities often include world-class processes, tighter control and reduced cycle time.

Once the business case is closed, companies often focus on software and not business objectives - with an implicit assumption that the benefits will follow. At this time, senior executives typically relegate too much responsibility to technical experts. They mistakenly view the endeavor as an information-technology project, not a business project.

Once management abdicates its responsibility for control, the working team is forced to make critical decisions by default.

Under this scenario, it is not long before the implementation begins to go off track. Well-intentioned people add "nice to have" functionality that can exponentially increase the level of complexity. Just getting to system cut over is a major accomplishment. Further complications are inevitable; it is common for an implementation to extend months beyond cut over because of unexpected problems such as missing data, slow response times or poorly trained staff.

Project managers sensing that budgets and schedules will soon far exceed original estimates try to get back on track by eliminating the redesign of certain business and physical processes. Implementation teams frantically tailor the new software to fit existing business practices. This rarely works.

As a result, the organization, having lost sight of any business objective, implements a crippled system, or one that is overloaded with unnecessary functionality. Whether the new system does not have enough capability nor has too much, the company now has a system that needs to be fixed. The process of upgrading or reworking is not only expensive; it is also almost too complicated to implement.

Given the investment required to implement new systems, why are senior managers not more involved? Our experience suggests that chief executive officers and top managers are simply unsure of the role they should play. Top executives and senior managers focus on objectives and issues, while systems experts focus on processes. Neither side can ask the right questions of the other.

Involvement by the chief executive officer on a small set of issues will greatly improve the likelihood of an implementation that is on budget and on schedule and that has the capabilities that support the corporate vision.

2.7.5 Involvement of the Chief Executive or the Division Manager:

The tope management need to be involved to take the following actions:

1. By clearly outlining the organization's strategic priorities;
2. By involving the organization at the appropriate level, and
3. By linking management controls and incentives to project success.

2.7.6 A Modest Formula for Reengineering

Reducing cost around machines requires reengineering of the process. One of the problems with reengineering is that there's no real formula for doing it. Every operation, every company, and every industry are different. Nonetheless, here's a short list of guidelines for getting results.

1. **Choose a process to reengineer:** It's often worthwhile to jumpstart the process by looking around for operations to improve.

2. **Create a reengineering team:** It should be composes mostly of people that work in that process (and in a variety of functions). You want buy-in from the people who will be involved, and they know better than anyone how things are currently done. Include someone with clout to clear away organizational roadblocks. Finally, if you can, put a person who has done the job elsewhere (or a consultant) on the team.

3. **Map the process:** Map it from start to finish in excruciating detail. Include branches or sub-processes.

4. **Improve the process:** You'll have to come up with measures that track the efficiency of the process as is and goals for what will be. Likely candidates include productivity measures, cycle times, and cost.

5. **Make sure your work pays off:** Reach your financial or productivity goals.

6. **Use Technology:** The experts agree on one point: Reinvent your process first, then use technology to speed it up or otherwise enhance the results you're seeking.

2.7.7 Identifying Cost Areas

When you begin to think of cutting waste, keep in mind the 80/20 rule. Also known as Pareto's Law or the rule of the trivial many and significant few, it says that 20 percent of the activities account for 80 percent of the results. The 80/20 rule applies to small operations as well as whole companies. That means 80 percent of your costs will come from 20 percent of the activities. Identify the cost spikes within your reach and see if you can lower them.

2.7.8 Cost Benefit Analysis

After identifying cost reduction projects, careful analysis to the most beneficial projects should be focused on.

2.7.9 Steps of Cost-benefit analysis:

1. Identification of relevant costs and benefits,

2. Measurement of costs and benefits,

3. Comparison of cost and benefit streams accruing during the lifetime of a project.

4. Priorities should be given to those projects that bring more savings with less effort and cost.

2.7.10 An Action Plan/ Getting Started

The most difficult step is simply to get started by overcoming the inertia present in any brown-field organization. Womack, J., and Jones, D., who wrote many subjects on lean thinking, recommend the following steps:

1. Find a change agent (Cost Reduction Coordinator) to lead the cost reduction effort.

2. Get the knowledge needed to lead the effort.

3. Find a lever by seizing the crisis, or by creating one

4. Forget grand strategy for the moment

5. Map your value streams: Once you've got the leadership, the knowledge, and the sense of urgency, it's time to identify your current value streams and maps them-activity by activity and step by step- by product family.

6. Begin as soon as possible with an important and visible activity

7. Demand immediate results

8. As soon as you've got momentum, expand your scope.

So basically, after empowering the Cost Reduction Coordinator and creating a sense of urgency for cost reduction, the cost reduction strategy will be simplified to each manager by expecting them to take the following steps,

2.7.11 Area Managers Action Plan:

1. Identifying the Cost Reduction Projects for different areas in the operation;

2. Prioritizing those 20% projects that bring 80% of the cost reduction results;

3. Implement these projects cautiously in order not to cause any interruption to the operation;

4. Monitoring the progress through a weekly, or biweekly meetings with area managers.

2.7.12 Evaluating Progress

Once companies commit to cost reduction, they spend a great deal of time and effort determining if the implementation is working. Manufacturing experts found that, even with cost reduction approach, a large-scale implementation has to take some senior management attention away from the business for a time. Problems always arise and organizational infighting can get out of hand.

Keeping the following in mind can assist in determining whether the implementation will succeed:

- Does top management understand the connection between the system implementation and the achievement of strategic goals well enough to describe the system's priorities in strategic terms?
- Is the implementation plan coherent, comprehensive and linked to corporate objectives and non- system-related capabilities?
- Does the process include dialogue and discussion about the hard choices necessary between the systems and other sources of control?
- Does the company buzz indicate the organization buys into the link between strategy and system implementation?
- These are key indicators that will help determine whether a cost reduction system will create a delivery system that runs like a dream, or a nightmare?

Because the goal of the team is to reduce costs from each line of the profit and loss statement, success can easily be measured by examining the next P&L. Once team members identify the line item dollars marked for reduction and put their plan in action, they can use each P&L statement as a monthly report card for tracking their progress. It is also important to track employees' performance against time. Keeping people on track by giving people deadlines for everything, then hold them to those deadlines. When you miss deadlines, costs mount.

2.7.13 Reasons for Becoming Lean

Researchers have found that the following factors directly affect an organization's ability to become lean. Companies must have:

- A strategic reason to pursue the lean path
- Active commitment of the top management team
- Cost reduction opportunity
- Growth potential
- Committed leaders of the company

It is not unusual for Productivity, Floor Space or Standard Work teams to create the following improvements in a short period of time:

- 25-35% productivity gain
- 50% floor space reduction
- 75% reduction in Work in Process

Team buy-in, commitment, and empowerment ensure long-term effective improvement activities. Periodically, the team is "huddled" together to discuss observations, try out new methods, and make operational/functional decisions. When the team and management agree upon a clear vision of improvements needed, a plan is developed to implement the improvements at the earliest opportunity. By setting the cost reduction target, and empowering the management team to pursue it, top management must look for a progress report periodically. In addition, top management needs to acknowledge progress, and reward achievers.

2.7.14 Next Steps for Lean Thinking

The fundamental issue facing senior management is to insure that high, and in certain cases; very high lean thinking generates full business benefits. The promise of the first wave of lean thinking has largely not been fulfilled. This is due not only to the problems in implementation of cost reduction projects, but problems were focused on fundamental organization structure and the need to timely implementation, and cost containment.

Persistence is one of the hallmarks of executives who are good cost cutters. They continually go back to their employees month after month, each and every year to remind them of the importance of cost reduction and tell them of their successes. They keep pursuing accounting and MIS to provide better information, and they continually use this information to identify areas of potential cot reduction. They continually find new ideas to keep cost management challenging and exciting.

2.7.15 Cost Reduction in Progress

CEO and Top Management Level:

- Lower your expectation of your total cost of manufacturing;
- Cut your budget in your all your business areas;
- Demand all managers of perspective areas to submit a plan to meet the new budget by distributing a balance percentage cut in all areas;
- Require a weekly or biweekly progress presentation by the Cost Reduction Coordinator;
- Set a reward for significant cost reduction results.

Managers Level:

- Identify and eliminate waste in all parts of your operation, and keep it in progress;
- Forecast more effectively with cost reduction in mind;
- Adjusting staffing levels;
- Reducing material acquisition cost;
- Reducing material inventory cost;
- Partner with your suppliers to save more money;
- Optimizing procurement efficiency;

- Optimizing factory utilization;
- Reducing manufacturing cost through cycle time;
- Reducing product development cost
- Reducing or eliminating discretionary activities;
- Reducing materials consumption and waste;
- Reducing travel costs;
- Reducing training costs;
- Improving company's information system to keep track of all cost reduction activities.
- Rewarding significant cost reduction results

CHAPTER 3

AN OVERVIEW OF THE TECHNIQUE

3.1 Introduction

The present book provides a mechanism to help identify cost reduction opportunities and structure cost reduction projects and provides techniques that help in the implementation of these projects. The technique aids the identification as well as the implementation of the cost reduction projects. It explains the methodology and the steps of the identification and implementation process of the cost reduction projects.

The current chapter provides an overview of the technique and the legitimate reasons why the technique has been developed. In addition, the procedures for the implementation of the technique are explained.

Besides taking a blue-sky method based on own experience, the author of this book is proposing state of the art techniques for identification and implementation of cost reduction projects for manufacturing companies. Companies in other industries may benefit from the concept and the technique to reduce their cost, and to stay lean.

In the subsequent section, the structure is presented and explained.

The technique comprises of five elements:

1. The appointment of the cost reduction management team,
2. Identification of cost reduction representatives from each department, and function area,
3. Assessment of the cost reduction target,
4. Identification of cost reduction projects, and
5. Implementation of the cost reduction projects.

The structure of the technique is explained in the following section.

3.2 Structure of the Technique

Several aspects distinguish cost reduction from the other cost cutting approaches. The first step of the technique is selecting and empowering the cost reduction team to drive the effort and be responsible for the ultimate result. The second step is identifying representatives from each department and manufacturing function area to manage cost reduction in their areas. The third step is setting the cost reduction target per department, and per function area. The fourth step is assigning responsibilities to each department and function area team to identify cost reduction projects in their area. The fifth step is implementing these cost reduction projects.

The cost reduction management team is responsible for the overall cost reduction target, monitoring the progress, and effectiveness of the cost reduction projects identification and implementation process. The management team tracks the progress by considering the identified cost reduction projects as potential savings, and considering the decrease in spending as actual savings. The projected saving and the actual savings are tracked in a spreadsheet format, and can be referred to as an action plan or a roadmap.

There are several considerations in managing cost reduction, which enhance the process of the technique:

1. Creating a team environment, and
2. Establishing a flow of communication to assist in identifying and implementing projects.
3. Presenting the cost reduction progress against target for each team in biweekly or monthly forums.
4. Presenting the progress reports in the presence of top management to ensure accountability, and timely accomplishment.

5. Besides meeting their weekly target, teams point out any risk or anticipated problem in the process, and any help needed.

Teams feel compelled to achieve their target and compete with other team for timely accomplishment. A diagram representing the structure of the technique is presented in Figure 3.2:

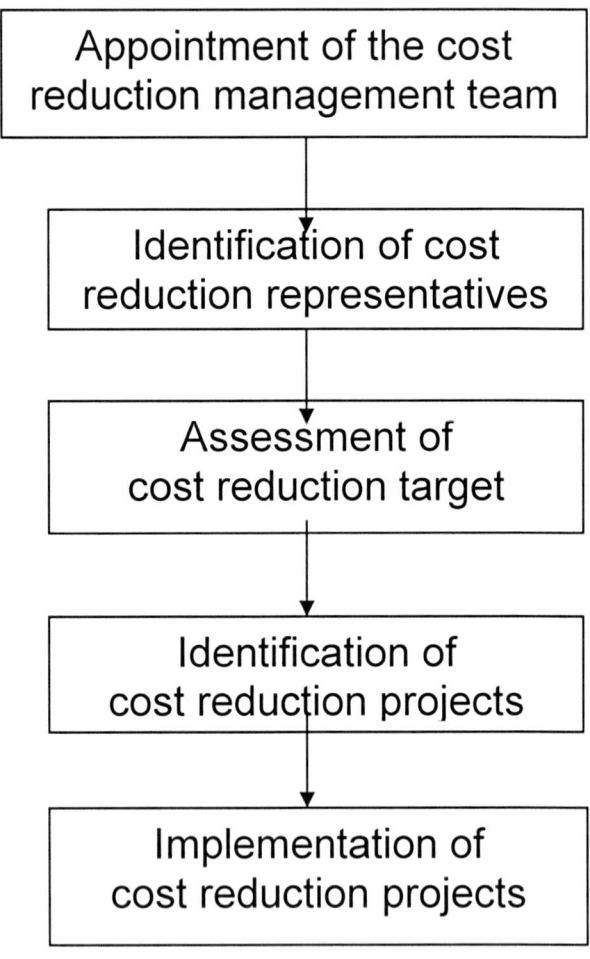

Figure 3.2 Structure of the technique

3.3 Procedure of the Technique

In order to prevent problems from occurring, the cost reduction tasks are generated through considering both the structures of the functional area teams and the manufacturing process. Furthermore, both the product aspects and the process aspects need to be considered throughout the processes of the cost reduction identification and implementation. Other consideration is given to the level of risk taking, the effect of these projects on quality of production, and the machine downtime.

3.4 Dividing the Target

The cost reduction target is divided into four major areas to be pursued by different departments and manufacturing function areas:

1. The first and the largest area is commodities, which includes saving opportunities in material such as spares, chemicals and gases, test tools, production material, metals, and miscellaneous commodities such as micros, probe cards and other manufacturing related commodities.
2. The second area is non-commodity, which includes direct and indirect labor, overtime, travel, training, recognition, supplies, relocation, consulting, and fixed spending.

3. The third area is a commercial saving, which includes alternative sourcing, referred to as direct sourcing, or second sourcing, and renegotiations of products' prices and service contracts.

4. The fourth area is a financial saving, which includes equipment and building depreciation, corporate expenses, tax write-offs, allocation, and applied judgment.

Projects will be identified and quantified in each manufacturing function area to support its cost reduction target.

The commodities' cost reduction projects are more engineering and technical in nature, which may include the reduction of preventive maintenance on tool sets, and machines. Using in house parts repair, and utilizing internal resources instead of paying extra for external resources will help reduce cost. In none commodity area, projects will include cutting the spending on overtime, travel, training, relocation, conserving power, telephone, pagers and office supplies. The commercial savings area, which deals with the supply chain channel, focuses on renegotiating prices on purchasing raw materials, spares, chemicals and gases, and any other material from alternative sources. This area requires the purchasing department to be more aggressive in obtaining lower prices through negotiation and finding quality supplies at cheaper prices. It also requires the purchasing department to maintain adequate inventory in order to avoid unnecessary cost of being over stocked, or pay a higher cost for rush delivery due to being under-stocked. A diagram representing the procedures of the technique is presented in Figure 3.3.

Cost Reduction Projects		
Project Area	**Project Classification**	**Project Type & Required Skills**
Commodity	A	Engineering and Technical
	B	
	C	
	D	
	E	
	F	
	G	
	H	
	I	
	J	
	Miscellaneous Commodities	
Non-Commodity	Direct and Indirect Labor Salaries	Negotiation
	Overtime pay	Reduce
	Benefits	
	Travel	Reduce to necessary
	Training	Business
	Recognition	Management
	Office Supplies	Contract
	Relocation Compensation	
	Consulting	Negotiation

	Fixed Spending	Reduce to necessary
	Utilities	Conserve power
	Telephone, and Communication	Reduce to necessary
	Insurance	Negotiation
	Security and Janitorial Services	
	Miscellaneous Non-Commodities	Reduce to necessary
Commercial	Alternative Sourcing	Business
	Negotiation of products prices	Negotiation
	Negotiation of service contracts	Purchasing
	Reduction of Inventory Build	Negotiation
	Reduction of Rush Delivery	
Financial	Building Depreciation	Financial
	Equipment Depreciation	
	Corporate Spending	Finance
	Corp. Building Depreciation	CPA
	Tax Write-Off and Judgment	CPA
	Allocations	Finance

Figure 3.3 Procedure of the technique

CHAPTER 4

DETERMINATION AND FORMULATION OF THE COST REDUCTION PLAN

4.1 Introduction

The detailed proposed techniques are discussed in this chapter. This discussion covers the Determination and setting of basic goals, the constitution of the cost reduction teams, the identification of the team interaction and communication, formulation of the cost reduction plan, and the implementation methodology.

Using state of the art techniques, a cost reduction roadmap is presented identifying basic goals for each area, department, and engineering team. Goals are assigned to each manufacturing area team, and department. The cost reduction management team should be in charge of leading, managing, supervising, coordinating and reporting the cost reduction activities.

For the identification of cost reduction target, appointment and empowerment of the management team, constitution of department and manufacturing areas teams, implementation of the cost reduction projects, the various categories concerning methods are discussed. The classification includes task types,

In the last section, strategies for managing the implementation of the cost reduction projects are suggested. Disseminating weekly report ensures the seriousness of the task; and keeps everyone informed of the progress. Meeting biweekly or monthly to report progress in a forum setting, where all representatives are present, ensures accountability, and update the progress toward achieving the cost reduction target. In these periodic meetings, in the presence of top management, cost reduction representatives communicate risks, opportunities, concerns and help needed.

4.2 Determination of Cost Reduction Target

In most cases, the overall cost reduction target can be set by the top management as a required goal in order to stay competitive or even to survive in a cut throat economy. In some cases however, the management ask the manufacturing team to determine a cost reduction target. In either way an astute cost reduction team will project the target or base it as a percentage of the overall spending.

Based on experience, the author of this book strongly believes that as a rule of thumb, manufacturing manufacturers can moderately reduce their cost 20% in the first year, 10% in the second year, and 5% in the third year. Considering the high annual spending of those manufacturers, cost reduction will result in a significant saving. As a realistic example, a small size manufacturing manufacturer spending is $500 Million a year. Applying the author's rule of thumb, cost reduction estimate will yield $100 Million saving in the first year, $50 Million saving in the second year, and $25 Million in the third year.

At any time during cost reduction, the target can be increased or decreased. Reasons for changing the target may include a change in the economy, risks, and opportunities. Companies avoid risks in regular environment; however in cost reduction mode there are risks associated with pursuing aggressive targets, risks in implementing engineering projects, and risks in loosing reliable suppliers.

On the other hand, there are opportunities that surface, discovered or learned while planning or implementing cost reduction projects. Getting all employees involved in cost reduction is an invitation to creativity, and out of the box thinking that bring new opportunities and result in unplanned saving.

4.3 Formulation of the Cost Reduction Plan

The cost reduction team set the cost reduction target based on the previous year's spending. It is more practical to communicate the cost reduction target in a dollar amount and as a percentage of the previous year's spending. The cost reduction management team will formulate an initial plan showing the target for commodity, non-commodity, commercial, and financial area. The plan also specifies name of owners, and deadlines for submitting planned and implemented projects that lead to meeting the targets. The management team may propose projects in broad terms; however, it is the responsibility of each department, and functional area to define projects that would lead to the initial target.

In the roadmap, the management team will show all the compiled plans received from various departments and functional area teams. The management team will check for gaps in the received plans, and revise the targets allocated to each team. The management team may increase or decrease targets as needed based on presented risks and opportunities.

Once a plan is determined to be realistic, scalable, and achievable, the cost reduction management team will get it approved by top management, communicate it to all teams, and move it into the implementation stage. See cost reduction roadmap in figure 4.5.

4.4 Formulation of the Implementation Methodology

A shared computer database is created to contain the commodity projects, non-commodity projects, and commercial projects. Due to the sensitivity, and confidentiality of the financial data, an update of the financial projects will be sent directly to the management team. Representatives from each team and department are granted access to make changes, and update cost reduction projects in their area. Every week, the management team analyzes the data, and formulates a weekly progress report, and disseminates it to the top management, and to the cost reduction representatives. In addition to disseminating the weekly progress report, the cost reduction stake holders hold biweekly or monthly forums to discuss issues related to the cost reduction planning, implementation, actual results, and level of confidence, risks, opportunities, and help needed to meet expectations. It is vitally important to communicate the importance of confidentiality of all cost reduction materials since they contain critical financial data, and strategies. See Appendix B for a sample of the cost reduction progress report.

The management team formulates a diagram to serve as an implementation plan depicting the flow of the implementation process, and time lines for updating the cost reduction roadmap, and presenting the progress in the cost reduction forum. The management team formulates revision 0 of the diagram, and sends it to all teams representatives to get their feedback and inputs. Keeping stakeholders engaged in all stages of cost reduction is an essential element of proper implementation methodology. Once the diagram is finalized, the management team will discuss it in the forum, and get it approved by top management.

See figure 4.4 for the implementation diagram.

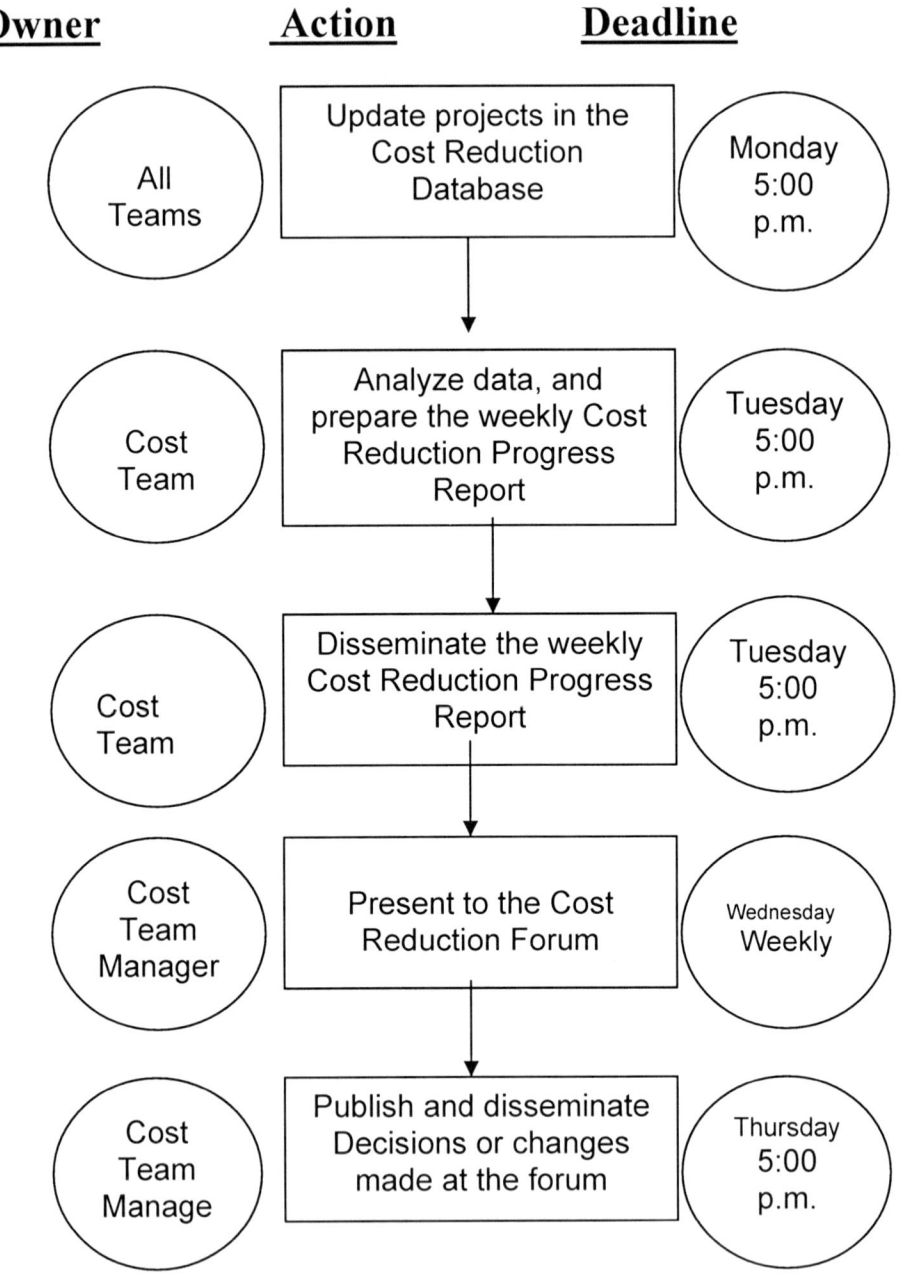

Figure 4.4 Implementation diagram

4.5 Monitoring the Cost Reduction Progress

It is essential to have all departments, and area teams work simultaneously, and to compare their progress against the progress of similar area team at other divisions. Teams' interaction maximizes the opportunities of learning about different projects. Sharing knowledge increases synergy throughout the process, and reflects positive impact on the organization. A cost reduction roadmap representing the flow of the process is presented in figure 4.5. Reviewing and updating the roadmap on weekly basis helps the management track the progress of the planning, implementation, and actual cost reduction projects. In addition, it helps the area team engineers to add and quantify new projects, and to re-quantify old projects in order to meet set expectation.

Concurrently, reviewing the roadmap weekly allows buyers to increase or decrease inventory build according to the need of stocking certain spare parts, chemical and gases, or needed test and production material. Also, reviewing the roadmap for preventive maintenance scheduling allows buyers to save money by using cheaper delivery method, and to order parts for tools that are still under warranty. See exhibit B for a sample of projects in a semi conductor company.

In order to attain cost reduction targets, dedication, persistence, expertise, accountability of the cost reduction team is essential, and recognition by top management is required. Cost reduction should be maintained, and the lean thinking should be implemented and monitored at all times.

Cost Reduction Roadmap

$ Per Million		Last Year	Cost Reduction Year #1 Target			Mid-Year Snap Shot				
						Cost Projects		Reduction		Gap: (Plan / Target)
Project Area	Project Classification	Spending	%	Spending	Reduction	Planned	Implemented	Actual	$	%
Commodity	A	70	30%	49	21	15	7	7	-8	47%
	B	50	20%	40	10	8	5	5	-3	63%
	C	15	20%	12	3	2	1.5	1.5	-0.5	75%
	D	60	10%	54	6	5	3	3	-2	60%
	E	2	10%	1.8	0.2	0.1	0.1	0.1	0	100%
	F	7	20%	5.6	1.4	1.2	1	1	-0.2	83%
	G	9	10%	8.1	0.9	0.6	0.4	0.4	-0.2	67%
	H	3	15%	2.55	0.45	0.4	0.3	0.3	-0.1	75%
	I	2	20%	1.6	0.4	0.3	0.2	0.2	-0.1	67%
	J	1.5	80%	0.3	1.2	0.9	0.8	0.8	-0.1	89%
	Miscellaneous Commodity	1	20%	0.8	0.2	0.1	0.05	0.05	-0.05	50%
$ Per Million	Sub-Total US$ in Millions	220.5	17%	175.75	44.75	33.6	19.35	19.35	-14.25	58%

Figure 4.5 cost reduction roadmap (part I)

Cost Reduction Roadmap

$ Per Million		Last Year	Cost Reduction Year #1 Target			Mid-Year Snap Shot				(Plan / Target)
						Cost Projects		Reduction	Gap:	
Project Area	Project Classification	Spending	%	Spending	Reduction	Planned	Implemented	Actual	$	%
Non-Commodity	Direct & Indirect Labor Salaries	80	10%	72	8	7	4	4	-3	57%
	Overtime Pay	7	50%	3.5	3.5	3	2	2	-1	67%
	Benefits	30	20%	24	6	4	4	4	0	100%
	Travel	1	70%	0.3	0.7	0.6	0.28	0.28	-0.32	47%
	Training	1	70%	0.3	0.7	0.5	0.56	0.56	0.06	112%
	Recognition	0.5	50%	0.25	0.25	0.1	0.1	0.1	0	100%
	Office Supplies	0.3	50%	0.15	0.15	0.1	0.1	0.1	0	100%
	Relocation Compensation	0.6	50%	0.3	0.3	0.25	0.16	0.16	-0.09	64%
	Consulting	0.4	50%	0.2	0.2	0.15	0.1	0.1	-0.05	67%
	Fixed Spending	0.3	20%	0.24	0.06	0.06	0.04	0.04	-0.02	67%
	Utilities	0.6	20%	0.48	0.12	0.11	0.06	0.06	-0.05	55%
	Telephone &	0.8	40%	0.48	0.32	0.31	0.19	0.19	-0.12	61%

Insurance	0.3	20%	0.24	0.06	0.05	0.04	0.04	-0.01	80%
Security & Janitorial Services	0.3	20%	0.24	0.06	0.1	0.02	0.02	-0.08	20%
Miscellaneous Non-Commercial	0.3	50%	0.15	0.15	0.2	0.1	0.1	-0.1	50%
$ Per Million Sub-Total	123.4	20%	102.83	20.57	16.53	11.75	11.75	-4.78	71%

Figure 4.5 cost reduction roadmap (part II)

Cost Reduction Roadmap

			Cost Reduction			Mid-Year Snap Shot				
		Last Year	Year #1 Target			Cost Projects		Reduction		
$ Per Million		Spending	%	Spending	Reduction	Planned	Implemented	Actual	Gap: (Plan / Target) $	%
Project Area	Project Classification									
Commercial	Alternative Sourcing:									
	Negotiation of Prod. Prices	180	20%	144	36	30	22	22	-8	73%
	Negotiation of Service Contracts	25	30%	17.5	7.5	5	3	3	-2	60%
	Reduction of Inventory Build	7	60%	2.8	4.2	3	2.5	2.5	-0.5	83%
	Reduction of Expedited Delivery	1	70%	0.3	0.7	0.5	0.4	0.4	-0.1	80%
$ Per Million Sub-Total		213	23%	164.6	48.4	38.5	27.9	27.9	-10.6	72%

Cost Reduction Strategies   Ammar Halloum

Financial									
	Building Depreciation/Appreciation	5	2%	4.9	0.1	0.07	0.04	0.04	-0.03	57%
	Equipment Depreciation	200	2%	196	4	3	1.6	1.6	-1.4	53%
	Corporate Spending	7	40%	4.2	2.8	2	1.8	1.8	-0.2	90%
	Corporate Building Depreciation/Appreciation	65	2%	63.7	1.3	1	0.36	0.36	-0.64	36%
	Tax Write-Off & Judgment	5	15%	4.25	0.75	0.7	0.28	0.28	-0.42	40%
	Allocations	45	15%	38.25	6.75	5	4.6	4.6	-0.4	92%
$ Per Million	Sub-Total	327	5%	311.3	15.7	11.77	8.68	8.68	-3.09	74%
$ Per Million	Total	540	12%	476	64	50	37	37	-14	73%

Figure   4.5   cost   reduction   roadmap   (part III)

CHAPTER 5

CONCLUSIONS AND FURTHER RESEARCH

5.1 Summary

A new approach has been presented to help the identification, and implementation of cost reduction opportunities. The objective of the presented technique is to help the transition from the traditional cost reduction approaches to the state of the art techniques. The new technique covers several fundamental requirements from team empowerment to team accountabilities. Actual application of the technique and its results has been tested at a manufacturing company. The validity and practicality of the technique have already been proven through the study presented in the previous chapter.

Through the work in this book, several important aspects have been recognized. The application of the technology, given a state of the art technique is explained. The contribution from the present research is discussed. In addition, possible further research issues are introduced for the establishment of more effective cost reduction identification, and implementation techniques in the future.

5.2 Conclusions

Transition from the traditional cost reduction techniques to the state of the art cost reduction technique can be established. This book provides a technique that helps the transition by investigating the requirements for the transition. Based on the research, the technique presented in this book is appropriate for helping manufacturers to reduce their cost by implementing this state of the art cost reduction system. Other companies can benefit from this research by applying the lean thinking, techniques, process, and methodologies. The non-commodity spending, the commercial spending and financial expenses are common denominators for most companies despite their size, and the industry they are in.

5.3 Contributions

The strategies, plans, and techniques in this book will contribute to manufacturing in particular, and to manufacturing in general in several ways. The aspect contributing to the present and future manufacturing is discussed.

The present technique simplifies and aids in identifying, and implementing cost reduction opportunities. The presented technique initiates the cost reduction system approach. It creates the environment for the improvement of effectiveness and efficiency in terms of time and cost.

The present research makes it possible to implement cost reduction, and achieve significant results in a fast time-cycle. The implementation integrates human resources, environment, time, cost, and quality. In the future, the cost reduction system will be used for planning and implementing more aggressive cost reduction, and to be useful for others who will be seeking future research.

5.3 Further Research

Through the development of the methodology associated with this book, the following possible future research issues have been recognized as a way to construct a different cost reduction system for different applications.

1. Conducting another study to focus on process engineering projects that lead to cost reduction for the manufacturing industry.

2. Develop software to be used as a model by different size companies.

3. Generalizing this research as basis for application by entities in the private as well as in the public sector.

****

REFERENCES

Eagle, F.A, 2001, 1st and 2nd stage commercialization guidelines: An indicator test for the commercialization of a traditionally manufactured product, University-of-Massachusetts-Lowell(0111),DD, pp 9, 343.

Hanover, B, 2002, Flexible Approaches to Implementing Lean Manufacturing, CCO,TPS-ThroughputSolutions-Manufacturing.Net,April,22, pp.1, 21, 27

Jackson,T,2000,GETTING 'LEAN' ISN'T EASY.(Implementing lean manufacturing reengineering), Industry Week, Jan, 13.

Johnson, Mark, A, 2001, Work Group Satisfaction As A predictor Of Total Productive Maintenance (TPM) Performance Outcomes, Wayne State University, Detroit, Michigan 18, DD (102), pp. 3, 8 , 13.

Kotter, John, P., 1996, Leading Change, pp. 10, 20.

Ludy, P. J., 2000, Profit Building: Cutting Costs without Cutting People, pp. 11, 27.

Meyer, C., 1993, Fast Cycle Time, How To Align Purpose Strategy And Structure For Speed, pp. 5

Micklethwait, J., and Wooldridge, A., The Art and Practice of Japanese Management, pp. 19

Montgomery, D., C., 1997, Design and Analysis of Experiments, pp. 33-34

Nas, Tevfik, F., 1996, Cost-Benefit Analysis, pp. 24.

Mora, E, and Castillo, A, 2001, Lean Strategies, Production Efficiencies Get a Foothold, Industrial Maintenance and Plant Operation, June, pp. 21.

Ohmae, Kenichi, 1982, The Mind of the Strategist, pp. 15.

Ohmae, Kenichi, The Godzilla Companies of the New Economy, pp. 9.

Olson, J., 1997, The Agile Manager's Guide To Cutting Costs, pp. 13, 15, 24, 27.

Rasch, S.F, 1998, LEAN MANUFACTURING PRACTICES: DO THEY WORK IN AMERICAN COMPANIES? (JOB SATISFACTION, PRODUCTIVITY) AU: RASCH-STEVEN-FREDERIC, THE-UNIVERSITY-OF-MICHIGAN (0127), DD 184, pp. 3.

Reeve, J.M., 2002, The Financial Advantages of the Lean Supply Chain: Supply Chain Management Review, March, pp. 15.

Richardson, P. R., 1998, Cost Containment: The Ultimate Advantage, pp. 28

Starns, J.F, 1995, A SYSTEMATIC APPROACH FOR ASSESSING MANUFACTURING CAPABILITY (INDUSTRIAL BASE, INFORMATION MANAGEMENT), THE-GEORGE-WASHINGTON-UNIVERSITY (0075), DD, 168: pp. 12

Stone, F. M. & Sachs, R. T., 1995, High-Value Manager: Developing the Core Competencies Your Organization Demands, pp. 20, 21.

The Witch Doctors, Times Books, 1996, How to Stop Bad Things from Happening to Good Companies, pp. 14, 16, 20, 21, 23.

White, J.H, 2000, Lean manufacturing: An industry wide study in application, California-State-University-Dominguez-Hills (0582), DD, 66.

Womack, J. P., Jones, D. T., 1996, Lean Thinking, Banish Waste And Create Wealth In Your Corporation, pp. 2, 10, 11, 25.

Womack, J. P., Jones, D. T. and Roos, D, 1990, The Machine That Changed the World: The Story of Lean Production, pp. 25.

Wu, Y.C.J, 1999, JUST-IN-TIME MANUFACTURING AND EXTERNAL LOGISTICS: EVIDENCE FROM AMERICAN PARTS SUPPLIERS, THE-UNIVERSITY-OF-MICHIGAN (0127), DD 166, pp. 17.

Appendix A
Sample of the Cost Reduction
Engineering Projects

Projects Roadmap

Tool Group	Project ID	Project Description	Commodity	Owner	Expected Completion Date	Annual Savings $
A	1	Extend exchange frequency	1		xx/xxxx	750,000
B	2	Extension of Preventive Maintenance	2		xx/xxxx	575,000
C	3	Utilizing more economic process	3		xx/xxxx	450,000
D	4	Replace with less specs, but still meet the industrial requirement	4		xx/xxxx	250,000
E	5	Extension of Preventive Maintenance	5		xx/xxxx	655,520
F	6	2x Extension of Preventive Maintenance	6		xx/xxxx	225,055
G	7	3x Extension of Preventive Maintenance	7		xx/xxxx	370,000
H	8	Re engineering of the process	8		xx/xxxx	150,000
I	9	Using less expensive material	9		xx/xxxx	755,750
J	10	Less power consumption	10		xx/xxxx	325,000

K	11	specialization	11		xx/xxxx	525,000
Total savings						5,031,325
This sample shows 11 engineering and business projects.						
An average size manufacturing manufacturer could easily develop 100 projects						

Sample of Cost Reduction Engineering and Business Project.

Progress Report on Engineering Projects

Progress Report, Work-Week 48

Tool Set/ Function	Saving Goals	Planned Projects	Implemented Projects	Gap to Goals	
	$/Million	$/Million	$/Million	$/Million	%
1	$9.50	$9.20	$8.75	-$0.50	95%
2	$9.10	$8.90	$8.46	-$0.20	98%
3	$8.25	$8.20	$7.79	-$0.05	99%
4	$7.50	$8.00	$7.40	$0.50	107%
5	$6.30	$6.20	$5.89	$0.00	100%
6	$6.05	$5.90	$5.61	-$0.25	96%
7	$5.80	$5.72	$5.53	-$0.08	99%
8	$5.40	$5.30	$5.13	$0.00	100%
9	$4.35	$4.25	$4.04	$0.00	100%
10	$3.25	$3.60	$3.24	$0.15	105%
11	$3.00	$2.95	$2.79	-$0.05	98%
12	$2.70	$2.70	$2.76	$0.00	100%
13	$2.45	$2.45	$2.14	$0.00	100%
14	$2.10	$2.10	$2.00	$0.00	100%
15	$1.90	$2.00	$1.90	$0.10	105%
16	$1.50	$1.49	$1.45	-$0.01	99%
17	$1.25	$1.23	$1.17	-$0.02	98%
18	$1.10	$1.25	$1.19	$0.15	114%
19	$0.90	$1.00	$0.92	$0.10	111%
20	$0.75	$0.75	$0.90	$0.10	112%
21	$0.70	$0.60	$0.57	$0.00	100%
22	$0.25	$0.26	$0.25	$0.01	104%
Totals	$84.10	$84.05	$79.85	-$0.05	100%

Progress Report on Engineering Projects

Appendix B
Sample of the Cost Reduction Progress Report.

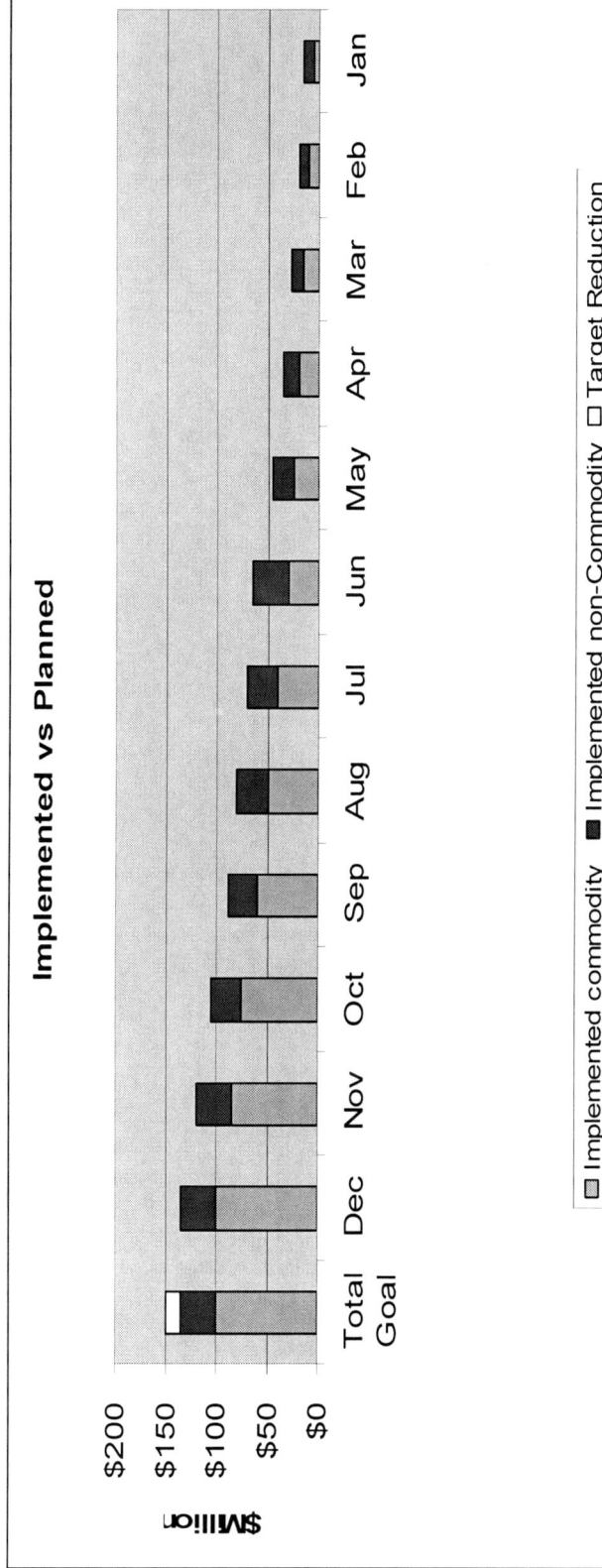

Publisher@atozpublisher.com
www.atozpublisher.com
ISBN: 978-0-9801197-1-8

Printed in the United Kingdom
by Lightning Source UK Ltd.
134375UK00002B/134/P